Handwriting Cursive Edition
Grades 2 and Up

SPEEDY
PUBLISHING

Speedy Publishing LLC
40 E. Main St. #1156
Newark, DE 19711
www.speedypublishing.com

Aa

Aa Aa Aa Aa Aa

Aa Aa Aa Aa Aa

$\mathcal{Bb}$

$\mathcal{Bb}$ $\mathcal{Bb}$ $\mathcal{Bb}$ $\mathcal{Bb}$ $\mathcal{Bb}$

$\mathcal{Bb}$ $\mathcal{Bb}$ $\mathcal{Bb}$ $\mathcal{Bb}$ $\mathcal{Bb}$

Cc

Cc Cc Cc Cc Cc

Cc Cc Cc Cc Cc

Dd

Dd Dd Dd Dd Dd

Dd Dd Dd Dd Dd

$\mathcal{E}e$

$\mathcal{E}e$ $\mathcal{E}e$ $\mathcal{E}e$ $\mathcal{E}e$ $\mathcal{E}e$

$\mathcal{E}e$ $\mathcal{E}e$ $\mathcal{E}e$ $\mathcal{E}e$ $\mathcal{E}e$

$\mathcal{G}g$

$\mathcal{G}g$ $\mathcal{G}g$ $\mathcal{G}g$ $\mathcal{G}g$ $\mathcal{G}g$

$\mathcal{G}g$ $\mathcal{G}g$ $\mathcal{G}g$ $\mathcal{G}g$ $\mathcal{G}g$

Hh

Hh *Hh* *Hh* *Hh* *Hh*

Hh *Hh* *Hh* *Hh* *Hh*

Li

Li *Li* *Li* *Li* *Li*

Li *Li* *Li* *Li* *Li*

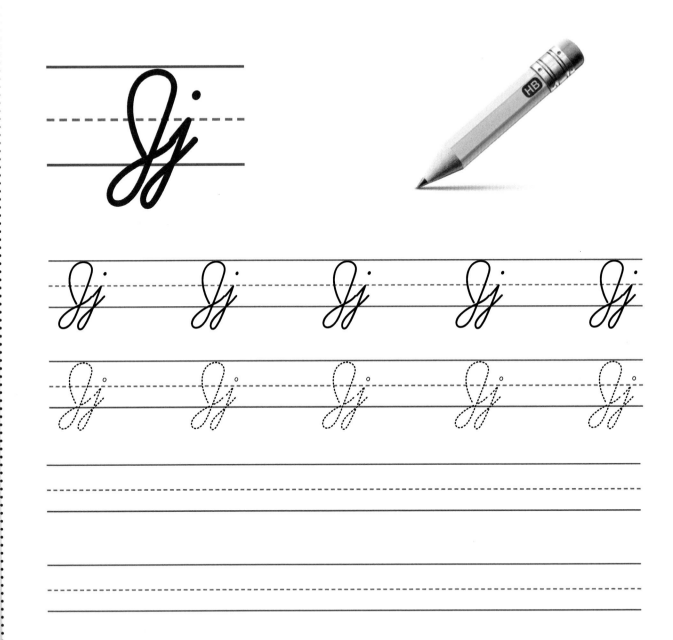

Kk

Kk Kk Kk Kk Kk

Kk Kk Kk Kk Kk

𝓛𝓵

𝓛𝓵   𝓛𝓵   𝓛𝓵   𝓛𝓵   𝓛𝓵

𝓛𝓵   𝓛𝓵   𝓛𝓵   𝓛𝓵   𝓛𝓵

$\mathcal{M}m$

$\mathcal{M}m \; \mathcal{M}m \; \mathcal{M}m \; \mathcal{M}m \; \mathcal{M}m$

$\mathcal{M}m \; \mathcal{M}m \; \mathcal{M}m \; \mathcal{M}m \; \mathcal{M}m$

Nn

Nn *Nn* *Nn* *Nn* *Nn*

Nn *Nn* *Nn* *Nn* *Nn*

Oo

Oo   *Oo*   *Oo*   *Oo*   *Oo*

Oo   *Oo*   *Oo*   *Oo*   *Oo*

$\mathcal{Pp}$

$\mathcal{Pp}$ $\mathcal{Pp}$ $\mathcal{Pp}$ $\mathcal{Pp}$ $\mathcal{Pp}$

$\mathcal{Pp}$ $\mathcal{Pp}$ $\mathcal{Pp}$ $\mathcal{Pp}$ $\mathcal{Pp}$

2q

2q   2q   2q   2q   2q

2q   2q   2q   2q   2q

$\mathcal{Rr}$

$\mathcal{Rr}$ $\mathcal{Rr}$ $\mathcal{Rr}$ $\mathcal{Rr}$ $\mathcal{Rr}$

$\mathcal{Rr}$ $\mathcal{Rr}$ $\mathcal{Rr}$ $\mathcal{Rr}$ $\mathcal{Rr}$

$\mathcal{S}s$ $\mathcal{S}s$ $\mathcal{S}s$ $\mathcal{S}s$ $\mathcal{S}s$

$\mathcal{S}s$ $\mathcal{S}s$ $\mathcal{S}s$ $\mathcal{S}s$ $\mathcal{S}s$

Tt

Tt Tt Tt Tt Tt

Tt Tt Tt Tt Tt

Ии

Ии Ии Ии Ии Ии

Ии Ии Ии Ии Ии

Vu

Vu   *Vu*   *Vu*   *Vu*   *Vu*

Vu   *Vu*   *Vu*   *Vu*   *Vu*

Ww

Ww Ww Ww Ww Ww

Ww Ww Ww Ww Ww

$\mathcal{X}x$

$\mathcal{X}x$ $\mathcal{X}x$ $\mathcal{X}x$ $\mathcal{X}x$ $\mathcal{X}x$

$\mathcal{X}x$ $\mathcal{X}x$ $\mathcal{X}x$ $\mathcal{X}x$ $\mathcal{X}x$

Yy

Yy *Yy* *Yy* *Yy* *Yy*

Yy *Yy* *Yy* *Yy* *Yy*

Zz

Practice Writing Numbers

One One One One One

One One One One One

Practice Writing Numbers

Two *Two* *Two* *Two* *Two*

Two *Two* *Two* *Two* *Two*

Practice Writing Numbers

Three Three Three Three Three

Three Three Three Three Three

Practice Writing Numbers

Four Four Four Four Four

Four Four Four Four Four

Practice Writing Numbers

Five Five Five Five Five

Five Five Five Five Five

Practice Writing Numbers

Six Six Six Six Six

Six Six Six Six Six

Practice Writing Numbers

Seven Seven Seven Seven

Seven Seven Seven Seven

Practice Writing Numbers

Eight   Eight   Eight   Eight

Eight   Eight   Eight   Eight

Practice Writing Numbers

Nine Nine Nine Nine Nine

Nine Nine Nine Nine Nine

Practice Writing Numbers

Ten   Ten   Ten   Ten   Ten

Ten   Ten   Ten   Ten   Ten

Practice Writing the Rainbow Colors

Red Red Red Red Red

Red Red Red Red Red

Practice Writing the Rainbow Colors

Orange Orange Orange Orange

Orange Orange Orange Orange

Practice Writing the Rainbow Colors

Yellow   Yellow   Yellow

Yellow   Yellow   Yellow

Practice Writing the Rainbow Colors

Green Green Green Green

Green Green Green Green

Practice Writing the Rainbow Colors

Blue Blue Blue Blue Blue

Blue Blue Blue Blue Blue

Practice Writing the Rainbow Colors

Indigo Indigo Indigo Indigo

Indigo Indigo Indigo Indigo

Practice Writing the Rainbow Colors

Violet   Violet   Violet   Violet

Violet   Violet   Violet   Violet

98248627R00029

Made in the USA
Lexington, KY
06 September 2018